A Year at St Gargoyle's

'Ron' is a real life parish priest in the Diocese of Salisbury. Hidden away in the depths of rural Dorset, he has created the zany, yet recognizably familiar world of St Gargoyle's, made famous by Ron's weekly cartoons in the *Church Times.*

Formerly a draughtsman, 'Ron' prefers to remain anonymous for the sake of his future career, but self-portraits appear regularly throughout this sparkling collection of cartoons ...

Also available from the Canterbury Press

The St Gargoyle's Calendar

Published in May each year, this wall-calendar will help you organize your life and keep you smiling throughout the year – all for £3.99!

To order your copy please send a cheque made payable to SCM – Canterbury Press Ltd, St Mary's Works, St Mary's Plain, Norwich NR3 3BH or fax your credit card (Visa or Mastercard) to 01603–624483.

A Year at St Gargoyle's

New Lectionary compatible!

Ron

as featured in the *Church Times*

CANTERBURY
PRESS
Norwich

Text and illustrations © Ron 1999

First published 1999 by The Canterbury Press Norwich
(a publishing imprint of Hymns Ancient & Modern Limited,
a registered charity)
St Mary's Works, St Mary's Plain,
Norwich, Norfolk NR3 3BH

British Library Cataloguing in Publication Data

A catalogue record for this book is available
from the British Library

ISBN 1–85311–315–8

Typeset by Rowland Phototypesetting Ltd,
Bury St Edmunds, Suffolk and
printed in Great Britain by
Biddles Ltd,
Guildford and King's Lynn

Introduction

Since I didn't think that the Archbishop of Canterbury would want to, I'm writing this myself. St Gargoyles cartoons began appearing in *Church Times* in September 1994 after our diocesan paper turned the series down. John Whale, who was *Church Times* Editor then, thought of the name, because he thought my idea, St Ickinsect, was silly!

Taking the mickey out of vicars, bishops and those small boys who carry candles is a centuries-old tradition of which I'm proud to be part. I'm a vicar myself, and every time I catch a glimpse of myself in a dog-collar it reminds me that God has a sense of humour.

None of the cartoons send up God. I won't have that. But cassocks, hassocks and wazzocks are fair game. There have still been a few complaints from irate readers, but most letters seem to be fairly appreciative. One rather worrying one came from a lady who said St Gargoyles gave her food for thought, which made me wonder whether she wasn't taking it too seriously. The cartoons appear in roughly chronological order through the Christian, rather than the calendar year, so can be taken as being 'New Lectionary compatible'.

One last point. There is no disclaimer in this book. Every cartoon is an accurate depiction of something that really happened to actual people. You know who you are.

Ron Wood

*The Misses Tredgett diced with
death playing chicken across the aisle.*

While the weathervane was being
mended, the churchwardens
improvised.

*They decided to try out all the
new Eucharistic prayers.*

The moral problems on genetic engineering were lost on the congregation.

*The problem of damp became
progressively worse.*

*Mrs Donovan could make up new hymn
tunes on the spot, and sometimes did.*

Miss Jones tried to enliven the
Litany with a Mexican wave.

The congregation braced herself for another little song from the Sunday school.

*The vicars and tarts party was
not a great success ...*

*Ian was named preacher of the year
at the insomniacs' gala dinner.*

*The bishop was cross because nobody
had told him it was fancy dress.*

The Revd. Nigel Pills believed in the power of prayer, but kept his options open.

'Read my lips', Wayne improvised, 'there
is NO room at the inn.'

*The man from C & A identified
the missing mannequins.*

The children found that daddy was free between midnight mass and the 8 o'clock service.

*The congregation joined in the familiar,
well-loved words of the vicar's
Christmas sermon.*

The choir outing went ahead, but
on a limited budget.

*Brian felt a strong calling to preach
to the people of Tahiti.*

*The church heating problem was
solved at last.*

On Monday nights they drank
gin and played schism.

*The vicar hoped people would stay for
a service after the coffee.*

*Michael dismissed St Valentine's Day
as mere commercialism.*

It was the vicar's day off, but there was no rest for the servers.

*The vicar announced that the choir
would sing Psalm 119.*

*Flowers were not allowed in church
during Lent.*

Charles began to have second thoughts about Midweek Sung Evensong during Lent.

The vicar had specially asked people to bring their mothers to church.

*Thomas opened the next door on his Lent
calendar, and put a chocolate in.*

It looked like a long night at the confessional.

Sir Rodney really enjoyed Easter Sunday.

There was some doubt as to whether the crops had actually been blessed.

*The Revd. Tobias Thring gave his team a
last-minute tactical briefing.*

The Revd. Habakkuk Wilkins was the victim of a bizarre meditation accident.

*Six out of ten people still preferred
the Book of Common Prayer.*

*The bishop's mother gave his nose
a quick wipe.*

*Nests under the eaves made Norman
think of Psalm 84.*

*Mrs Stebbings always did the flowers
in the south window, as Mrs Todger
soon learned.*

He regarded the Woods as a real
feather in his cap.

*The Revd. Attila T. Hun gave way to
an ancestral urge.*

40,321 changes of Plain Bob Major
was a new world record.

*The man from the council came to
deal with the cassock weevil.*

*Without the mice, Nesbit's role
became purely ceremonial.*

After a long hard debate the PCC rushed for the Division Lobbies.

*The inventory seemed complete
except for one almsdish (pewter).*

The churchwardens perfected their routine for the Archdeacon's visitation.

*Humphrey had an emergency meeting
with the Diocesan arsonist.*

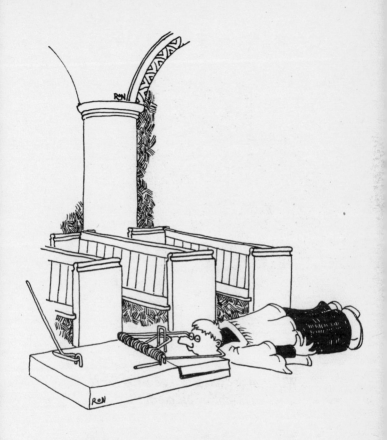

*The church mice exacted a terrible
revenge.*

*William realised it was time for a
firm policy on confetti.*

Simon led the march of wetness.

*Kevin's sermon illustration for
Trinity Sunday was particularly
unlucky.*

Father Charles had thought it was only Thursday.

*Young Lawrence became a victim of
the Whoopee Hassock.*

Mr Steel made it quite clear he
did not want to share the peace.

The sidesmen were pleased to report an increase in the weekly offerings.

The vicar said the service sheets
were not to be taken away.

*The new curate was a little
shy at first.*

*Roderick tried to impress Belinda
with his fluent greek.*

*Robert prayed for all the Spice Girls,
or, failing that, any one of them.*

'And now we'll try a new song,' said Trevor –
'It's called "Kumbaya".'

*Not everyone appreciated
the vicar's little jokes.*

*Peter wore a special dog-collar
to stop him scratching.*

The boy sopranos cured the rector's hiccups.

*After an embarrassing delay, the
nun was helped from the cake.*

The choir simply ignored the ban on bubble gum.

*In remote parishes, the mobile service
was appreciated.*

'Now try it again', suggested the bishop,
'with me INSIDE.'

*Clergy about to retire are
given essential re-training.*

The thing in the font had claimed another victim ...

*The painter didn't stop at the
downpipes and gutters.*

*They replaced the old organ with the
finest electronic they could afford.*

Sir Roland's nose had been restored in the gothic style.

'Last one there stinks!' cried the boat boy,
breaking into a run.

Mrs O'Leary was a black belt at ikebana.

*Father Rupert described himself as a modern
Anglo-Catholic.*

Godfrey apologised, but the damage was done.

*Alan suffered the twin curse of the
N.S.M. – overwork, and no real status.*

*The Procession followed
the Crucifer in a dignified
manner.*

*Brother Chuck Lumps, from Utah, was
confounded by sound Anglican
theology.*

Father Peter thought of a plan to keep all his other Saturdays free.

*Derek found his position usurped
by a quota-hopping Spanish priest.*

*There were seminars in clinical theology,
preaching in the new millennium, and
line dancing.*

'Oh yes?' retorted Thomas, 'well, my
archdeacon could thrash your archdeacon!'

On our planet there is only one sex, the sky is pink, and we smile as we share the peace.

*So where, wondered the bishop's wife,
was her novelty oven-glove?*

*Even the bishop's chaplain, whose tact
was legendary, found the oven-glove
a problem.*

*The game of spillikins had been planned
as light relief.*

*Unthinking, Barry knocked out his pipe
on the bishop's tortoise.*

*It was a day of great rejoicing – there were
no pesetas in the collection.*

*The churchyard regulations were not
always strictly enforced.*

The churchyard was managed to encourage wildlife.

*At twenty pence, trips up the
tower were a bargain.*

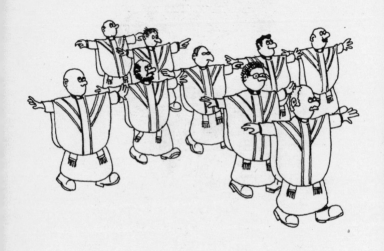

*The fete concluded with a death-defying
display by the crack formation team,
the 'Red Chasubles'.*

But inside, it was still St Willibert's.

*The Reverend Peter Worms praying
for Great Britain at the summer Olympics.*

*Conrad was pleased to see the
Toronto Blessing in Skegness.*

Blessing the guillemots was a tough job,
but somebody had to do it.

*The sisters came back from
Japan transformed.*

'Tell me again,' said the visitor, 'about this
Apostolic Succession.'

*In 2295 AD, the annual meeting of the A.S.B. Society
was held on one of Jupiter's moons.*

*The monks accepted a generous
sponsorship deal.*

*Even after he retired, the Revd. Nutleg would
forget himself and drink the washing-up water.*

*The oasis broke out of the cupboard
and engulfed Mrs McCredy.*

*William began to regret asking daddy
to help with his R.E. homework.*

As the vicar alarm went off,
the Robinsons dived for cover.

*The crypt lay hidden for centuries, until
one harvest festival ...*

*Brewing his own Communion wine proved
a false economy, Bertram concluded.*

*The enactment of the Tower of Babel
ended predictably in tears.*

*George practised the laying on of hands
with prayer.*

*At last the search for a new
organist was over.*

*Not everyone was against having
girls in the choir.*

'Strictly speaking', said the Archdeacon,
'you should have applied for a faculty.'

*The Revd. Stavely Grout enthralled
his grandchildren with tales of
General Synod.*

The man from Guinness verified it as the world's largest hassock.

'I hate it when this happens,'
said Toby.